THE KOREAN WAR

TOM McGOWEN

THE
KOREAN
WAR

FRANKLIN WATTS

New York ★ Chicago ★ London ★ Toronto ★ Sydney

A First Book

TO CHRISTOPHER

(Frontispiece) A soldier comforts a grief-stricken infantryman whose friend had been killed in action in Korea in the summer of 1950.

Maps by William J. Clipson

Cover photograph copyright © Devaney Stock Photos

Photographs copyright © : Veterans of Foreign Wars: chapter openers; PHOTRI: p. 2; UPI/Bettmann Newsphotos: pp. 9, 18 top, 20 top, 28, 47, 50, 55 top; The National Archives: pp. 12, 20 bottom, 22, 25, 36, 52 bottom, 54; United Nations Photos: pp. 18 bottom (Anpfoto), 19 top, 44 top (both U.S. Army), 19 bottom, 53 bottom; AP/Wide World Photos: pp. 37 top, 42, 44 bottom; Sovfoto/Eastfoto: pp. 37 bottom, 41, 45 top; Journalism Services/Bob MacDonald: p. 45 bottom; FPG International: p. 52 top; U.S. Army Photo/Cpl. J.J. McSinty: p. 53 top; Korea National Tourism Corporation: p. 55 bottom.

Library of Congress Cataloging-in-Publication Data

McGowen, Tom.
The Korean War / by Tom McGowen.
p.   cm. — (A First book)
Includes bibliographical references and index.
Summary: An overview of the three-year war that took over two million lives and resolved none of the conflicts that split Korea into two irreconcilable nations.
ISBN 0-531-20040-X (lib. bdg.) / ISBN 0-531-15655-9 (pbk.)
1. Korean War, 1950-1953—Juvenile literature.   [1. Korean War, 1950-1953.]   I. Title.   II. Series.
DS918.M38   1992
951.904'3—dc20   91-14747 CIP AC

CONTENTS

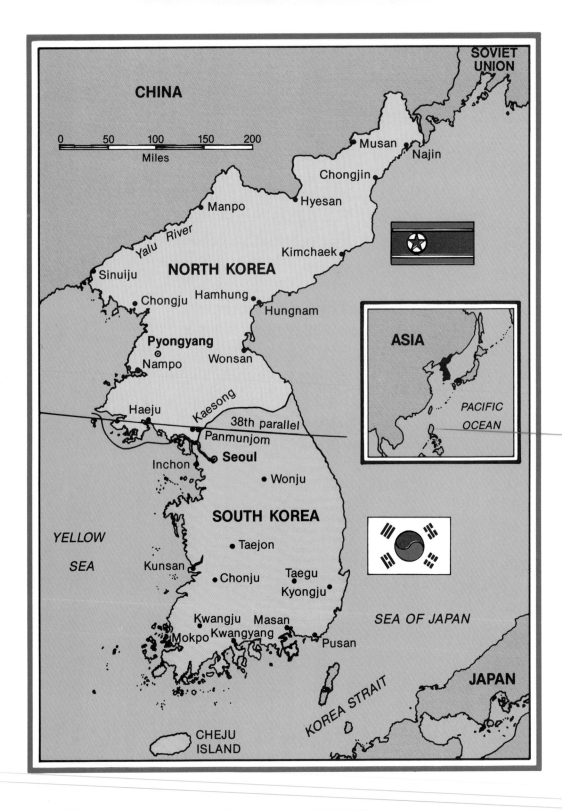

ONE

THE INVASION OF SOUTH KOREA

KOREA is a long, narrow piece of land that sticks down out of northern Asia into the sea. It is a land of hills and high mountains, deep valleys, broad rivers, and many tiny villages. Its summers are hot and wet; its winters bring bone-chilling cold and snow. Except for a tiny bit in the northeast that is bordered by the former Soviet Union, the northern border of Korea rests against the northern part of the huge land of China. To the west, across a stretch of sea, lies central China, and to the east, across another small stretch of sea, lie the islands of Japan.

Korea is the home of more than 60 million people who, to westerners, seem to resemble their Chinese and Japanese neighbors, but are really quite different in a number of ways. Most of them are farmers, growing crops of rice, soybeans, and barley.

From time to time since the 1400s, Korea has been invaded and conquered by either China or Japan. From 1910 to 1945 it was completely under Japanese control, governed by Japanese officials and occupied by soldiers of the Japanese army. When World War II ended in 1945 with the defeat of Japan by the United States and its allies, Korea was abruptly on its own. It had no government and no money—not even a native police force or army. The United States and the Soviet Union, which were then allies, agreed that Soviet troops would temporarily occupy and aid the part of Korea north of the 38th parallel (an artificial map line that cuts the country almost exactly in half), while U.S. troops would occupy and aid the part south of the 38th parallel.

Soon after the end of World War II, the alliance between the United States and the Soviet Union began to crumble. The Soviet Union was vigorously trying to establish its form of government, communism (a system in which the government maintains strong control over peoples' lives), in other nations. In China, Greece, and other places, Communist revolutionary armies supplied and aided by the Soviet Union waged civil war to take control of their countries. The United States and its western allies watched these events with growing alarm. To them it seemed as if the Soviet Union were actually attempting to take over the whole world with communism.

In 1947 the United Nations called for an election to be

Rice paddies separate these two tiny farming villages – the "Freedom Village" (foreground) in South Korea, and the "Peace Village" (background) – in North Korea. Located on the heavily guarded border between North Korea and South Korea, the two villages have not communicated since the country was divided into two separate nations in 1953.

held in Korea to establish a single government. The Soviet Union, however, refused to allow any election to be held in the north.

In 1948 Soviet troops were withdrawn from the north, which had been turned into a fervent Communist nation calling itself the Democratic People's Republic of Korea. Soviet military experts had trained an efficient North Korean army, and the Soviet Union had armed it with tanks, airplanes, and modern weapons.

In 1949 the U.S. troops left the south. The region had become modeled after a Western democracy like the United States or Canada, with political parties, a president, and a "congress" of representatives of the people. It called itself the Republic of Korea. American military specialists had trained an army for South Korea, but it was far less well equipped than the Soviet-backed army of North Korea.

Thus, there were now two separate nations on the land of Korea, and the governments of these nations thoroughly detested each other. Each government claimed that only *it* truly represented all Korea and that the other government was false. There was constant tension between the two nations.

In October 1949 the civil war in China ended with a victory for the Communist forces, and the vast land of China became a Communist nation. Now, North Korea had two mighty allies to back it, China and the Soviet Union.

On the morning of June 25, 1950, with the claim that they were defending their nation against a sneak attack by South

Korean forces, advance units of the 135,000 soldiers of the North Korean army poured over the 38th parallel, invading the south. The troops of the Republic of Korea (ROK) that moved against the invaders were badly outnumbered and outclassed. By the next day much of the South Korean army had been destroyed, and North Korean troops were moving unopposed toward Seoul, the capital of South Korea, to capture it. It was obviously the intention of the North Korean leader, Kim Il Sung, to conquer the south and unify the entire country under his Communist government.

The United States was outraged. It still considered itself responsible for the well-being of South Korea. To the United States and its western allies this attempt to take over South Korea and turn it to communism by force was a challenge to democracy and freedom and a threat to law and order in the world. The United States government quickly urged the Security Council of the United Nations (UN) to meet and vote on a resolution ordering North Korea to withdraw its army from the south. Had the Soviet ambassador to the UN been at the meeting, he would have been able to prevent such a vote, according to UN rules. However, he had been temporarily withdrawn by his government as a protest because the UN would not accept members from Communist China. The resolution passed, nine votes to none.

North Korea, however, simply ignored the UN demand. The UN Security Council now asked members of the United Nations to give military aid—supplies, weapons, and

Kim Il Sung, leader of the North Korean Communist government and commander in chief of the North Korean People's Army

Shortly after the North Korean army overran the South Korean capital of Seoul, President Harry S. Truman sent American troops into the city of Pusan. They were instructed to move north and engage the enemy in battle.

troops—to the Republic of Korea to help it halt the invasion. Many members, including Britain, Canada, Australia, New Zealand, and France, instantly pledged help. But the nearest troops belonging to a non-Communist member nation of the UN were those of the United States, stationed in Japan under the command of General of the Army Douglas MacArthur.

Thus, the United States became the first UN member actually to go to South Korea's aid. On June 27, President Harry S. Truman authorized U.S. Air Force and naval forces to help South Korea, and on June 30, two days after North Korean troops had captured Seoul, Truman authorized American troops to be sent to Korea. The next day, the U.S. Twenty-fourth Infantry Division (about 12,000 men) began leaving Japan for Korea.

The United States had not actually declared war on North Korea. As one American senator put it, sending U.S. military forces to Korea was "a police action against a violator of the law of nations." So, the war that was to be officially known as the "Korean Police Action" was about to begin.

THE FIGHT
FOR PUSAN

THE FIRST portion of the Twenty-fourth Infantry Division to reach Korea was two-and-a-half companies of a battalion of the Twenty-first Infantry Regiment, accompanied by six howitzers (cannons) and their crews, a total of some 540 men.

The Korean city of Pusan, to which this unit was flown, was vitally important. It was a major port at the southern tip of South Korea, and it possessed an airfield. Thus, it was an ideal place for the United Nations military force to land troops and supplies and to use as a base for carrying on a war in Korea. However, if the North Korean army captured Pusan, the UN forces would have to create a base somewhere else by landing troops and supplies somewhere on the coast, building an airstrip, etc. — a long, difficult, and very dangerous operation. So it was the job of that little American unit of 540 men — commanded by Colonel Charles Smith and known as "Task Force Smith" — to keep any North Korean troops from getting to Pusan until there were enough UN troops in the city to defend it from capture. By train and trucks, Smith's little force moved northward until it reached a place where three hills overlooked the road that ran from Seoul to Pusan, down which any North Korean troops would come. There Smith put his men in place to dig in and await the enemy.

When World War II had ended five years earlier, the United States had the most powerful military forces in the world. But this condition had been allowed to deteriorate since that time. In 1950, most young soldiers making up the combat forces of the U.S. Army were poorly trained, inexperienced, and lacked the up-to-date weapons needed for modern warfare. Nevertheless, most American military and political leaders felt that just the presence of a small U.S. force in Korea would be enough to "scare off" the North Korean troops. Indeed, most American soldiers believed that the Koreans, whom they contemptuously called "gooks," would be no match for them. Thus, both the soldiers of Smith's task force and the generals who had sent them felt fairly sure that Task Force Smith would be able to halt the North Korean advance.

They were wrong. On July 5, when the North Korean force that had been sent to capture Pusan reached the place where Colonel Smith's troops were waiting, the North Koreans did not hesitate. Not only was Smith's force badly out-

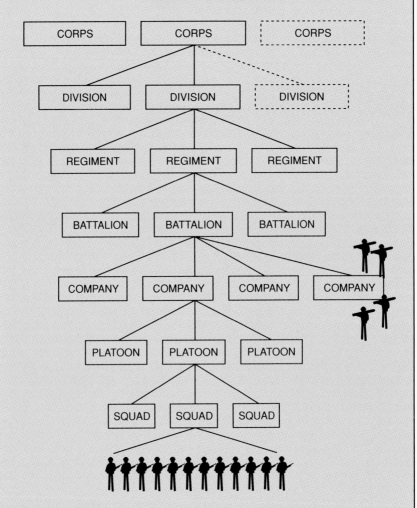

ARMY

CORPS — CORPS — CORPS

DIVISION — DIVISION — DIVISION

REGIMENT — REGIMENT — REGIMENT

BATTALION — BATTALION — BATTALION

COMPANY — COMPANY — COMPANY — COMPANY

PLATOON — PLATOON — PLATOON

SQUAD — SQUAD — SQUAD

An army is composed of many different groups of soldiers who are joined together to form larger groups. In 1950, a U.S. infantryman, or foot soldier, was a member of a *squad* of twelve riflemen. Three such squads formed a *platoon*. Three platoons made up a *company*. Three companies of riflemen, plus companies armed with high-caliber machine guns and other large weapons, made up a *battalion*. Three battalions formed a *regiment*. Three regiments were grouped together to make a *division* (about 16,000 men, at full strength). Two or more divisions were grouped together to form a *corps,* and an *army* was made up of two or more corps plus divisions.

numbered, but it also had no weapons of the sort needed to fight off tanks, of which the North Koreans had thirty-three. As the big, green Soviet-built tanks moved right through Smith's men, the North Korean soldiers spread out and moved around to hit the Americans from both sides. Within a few hours, Task Force Smith was in full retreat, having lost more than one-third of its men. The United States had been soundly beaten in its first encounter with North Korean troops.

By now, the rest of the Twenty-fourth Division had arrived in Korea. Its commander, Major General William Dean, quickly placed his soldiers, and all the ROK troops available to him, into position to hold off the oncoming North Korean advance. But, usually outnumbered in battle and still with few or no weapons to fight off tanks, the American and ROK battalions were badly demoralized and seemed unable to stand against the enemy. They were steadily pushed back. On July 19, in a bitter battle within the burning city of Taejon, north of Pusan, the entire Twenty-fourth Division was forced into headlong retreat. General Dean was cut off from escape and eventually captured. It was a stunning defeat.

However, the soldiers of the Twenty-fourth Division had managed to hold off the North Korean advance for several days. Meanwhile, more and more troops, including a small British force, had landed at Pusan. Under the command of American lieutenant general Walton Walker, this UN

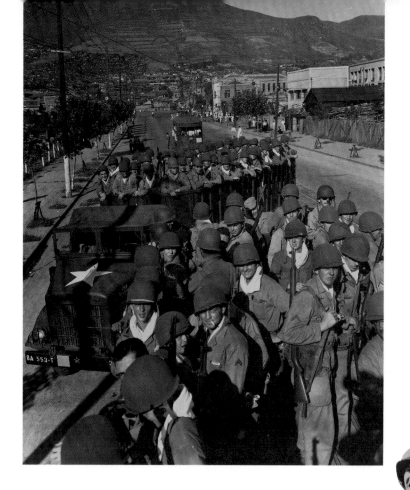

Defenders of South Korea.
Clockwise, from top left:
Fresh U.S. marine troops
arrive in Pusan. Soldiers
of the Republic of Korea
Army stand at attention
during a military inspection.
Dutch and Thai soldiers
serving in the UN army
befriend each other before
going into battle. A Dutch
soldier models his
equipment.

army, designated the "Eighth Army," formed a ring of defense around the city. In addition to thousands of soldiers, there were tanks, heavy artillery, and aircraft.

The North Korean forces began a series of vicious attacks to break through the "ring" and take Pusan. Several times they nearly succeeded, but the UN soldiers managed to fight off every push, poke, and thrust the North Koreans made. However, it was clear that the supposedly mighty forces of the United States and its UN allies were barely able to hold out against the troops of a small, third-rate power.

Then, General MacArthur, who on July 7 had been appointed Supreme Commander of UN forces, made a move that suddenly changed the entire course of the war.

Facing page, top: Major General William Dean, commander of the Twenty-fourth Infantry Division. *Facing page, bottom:* Lieutenant General Walton Walker, commander of the UN Eighth Army that defended Pusan from a vicious North Korean offensive

General Douglas MacArthur (wearing dark glasses) and his party tour a United States-occupied section of Korea.

THREE

THE LANDING AT INCHON

GENERAL Douglas MacArthur was a clever strategist. He had commanded the American forces in the southwest Pacific in World War II in the operations against Japan. What MacArthur did now was to work out a plan for UN forces to move into South Korea behind the North Korean army that was advancing on Pusan. This would cut off the North Korean army from its source of supplies and trap it between two UN forces.

MacArthur intended to land troops at the port city of Inchon on Korea's west coast, some 20 miles (32 km) from Seoul. But there were many risks to his plan. Inchon was in territory held by North Korea. There were North Korean troops there, which meant the UN landing force would have to fight its way ashore. The channel, or stretch of water leading to the landing area, was narrow and twisted. If the North Koreans had mined the channel with floating explosives, ships carrying UN troops could be damaged and sunk.

And, there was Wolmi-do Island, a small fortified island offshore, which the UN ships would have to pass, and they could be damaged and destroyed by artillery fire from it.

Because of all these problems, the generals and admirals in charge of the U.S. Army, Navy, and Marine Corps were opposed to MacArthur's plan. For six weeks they and MacArthur argued and wrangled over it. During that time, the UN Eighth Army troops around Pusan were desperately fighting to hold off the North Koreans. Finally, MacArthur got his way. Troops and ships were assembled and the landing force, labeled the "Tenth Corps," sailed to its destination.

On September 10, 1950, the assault began. Marine and navy planes roared over Wolmi-do Island, raining down fire bombs. Buildings, trees, bushes, and grass exploded into flames. American and British warships sailed into the channel. After destroying the floating mines with gunfire, they turned their guns on the fortified island and attacked, smashing any North Korean artillery that tried to fire back. On the morning of September 15, with marine planes flying low ahead of them and spraying the ground with machine-gun fire, a battalion of the Fifth Marine Regiment stormed onto the island and swept forward, wiping out all opposition. Within an hour the island was captured, and the way to Inchon was clear.

At 3:30 that afternoon, the attack on Inchon began. Men of the First and Fifth Marine Regiments and a ROK marine

On September 15, 1950, men and equipment were unloaded off four battleships during the amphibious landing at the port city of Inchon.

regiment charged out of their boats toward the 15-foot (4.6 m) high wall that blocked their path to the city. In some places they climbed it with ladders; in others, they blew holes in it with dynamite and crawled through. Once past the wall, the marines met a hail of bullets from North Korean soldiers in trenches and behind barricades. The marines charged, and the enemy soldiers surrendered or turned and ran. By six o'clock, U.S. marines were swarming through Inchon, and there was no further resistance. MacArthur's plan was a success.

Once Inchon was firmly under control, the UN force launched an attack toward Seoul to retake that city from the North Koreans. The U.S. First, Fifth, and Seventh Marine Regiments and the Thirty-second Infantry Regiment, together with ROK units, moved against Seoul from two directions, fighting continuous, bitter battles against North Korean troops all the way, mile after mile and hill after hill. Marines moving up from behind passed the dead bodies of marines who had fought ahead of them.

Most of these young soldiers were as poorly trained and inexperienced as the first Americans in Korea had been, only now they were well equipped and had the help of tanks and aircraft. The small units of North Korean troops being thrown desperately against them could slow them down, but not stop them. However, the Americans were finding out, as one young soldier said, "there is no glory in war. It's cruel, miserable, dirty, and nothing worth bragging about."

In Seoul, North Korean soldiers barricaded the streets and hid inside buildings, firing down from windows. American soldiers had to fight their way from street to street, throwing hand grenades into buildings and moving cautiously behind tanks that smashed through the barricades. Because of this kind of fighting, much of the city was destroyed. But by September 28, Seoul was under UN control; the defeated North Koreans had pulled out of it and were fleeing northward.

Meanwhile, in the south, the UN army in a ring around Pusan had, on September 16, begun a strong push against the North Korean force facing it. This push was timed to coincide with the landing at Inchon; the UN leadership believed the North Korean troops in the south would be called back to Seoul when the landing began and the way would be clear for the Eighth Army to move out after them. However, the North Korean army had not been notified of the landing and had stayed right where it was, so the UN soldiers found themselves engaged in vicious fighting, able to move forward only very little or not at all.

But within a few days the North Koreans learned that Inchon and Seoul had fallen and that their army was cut off. Some North Korean troops surrendered, some remained to fight until they were overwhelmed, but most turned and began to head back north. They were vigorously pursued by U.S., British, and South Korean troops of the Eighth Army and were under constant attack from U.S. aircraft.

Soon, the North Korean army simply began to break apart, turning into thousands of little groups of desperate men with no goal but to somehow get back across the 38th parallel to the safety of North Korea. Many of these men were killed or captured. Of roughly 70,000 North Korean soldiers involved in the battle for Pusan, no more than 25,000 to 30,000 managed to get back to the north, by way of back roads and mountain paths that hadn't been blocked by UN troops. By September 29, the only North Korean soldiers left in the south were prisoners. It seemed South Korea was free once again.

A few yards from where his comrade lies dead (left background), a North Korean soldier crawls away from a group of gun-toting U.S. marines during the recapture of Seoul in September 1950.

FOUR

CHINA ENTERS THE WAR

ALTHOUGH the United States and its allies had done what they set out to do — keep South Korea from being conquered — the Korean problem was far from solved. North Korea had not surrendered, so the war was not over. The North Korean army had been badly damaged but not totally destroyed. It was still a threat.

The United States and most of its allies believed that North Korea had to be prevented from causing any more trouble. Many people — General MacArthur among them — thought the UN should conquer North Korea and turn all of Korea back into a single nation under the control of the South Korean government. Others feared that if UN troops invaded North Korea to conquer it, China, and perhaps the Soviet Union, might enter the war to help the North Koreans. Such a turn of events could lead to World War III!

After much consideration and consultation with allied leaders, the Truman administration decided to permit General MacArthur to send the UN army across the 38th parallel into North Korea to destroy the North Korean Army. However, MacArthur was directed to allow only ROK troops, and no Americans, to go into the northernmost part of North Korea, along the Chinese border. This was intended to show the Chinese that the United States was not trying to threaten them.

But the Chinese did feel threatened. Relations between the United States and China were very poor at this time, for the United States was opposed to the Communist government that had taken over China. The United States supported the former government, which the Communists had driven out and which had taken refuge on the island of Taiwan, off the Chinese coast, under American protection. The Chinese Communist government feared that if North Korea were conquered, the United States might use it as a base to wage war against China to put the old government back in power. Thus, the Chinese Communists believed they simply could not allow North Korea to be conquered.

Knowing that his words would be reported to the United States government, one of the Chinese leaders, Zhou Enlai, told an ambassador from India that if American troops crossed the 38th parallel, China would enter the Korean War. Unfortunately, this warning was ignored by American government officials. On October 9, 1950, General Walker's Eighth Army, which was made up mainly of Americans, crossed the 38th parallel into North Korea.

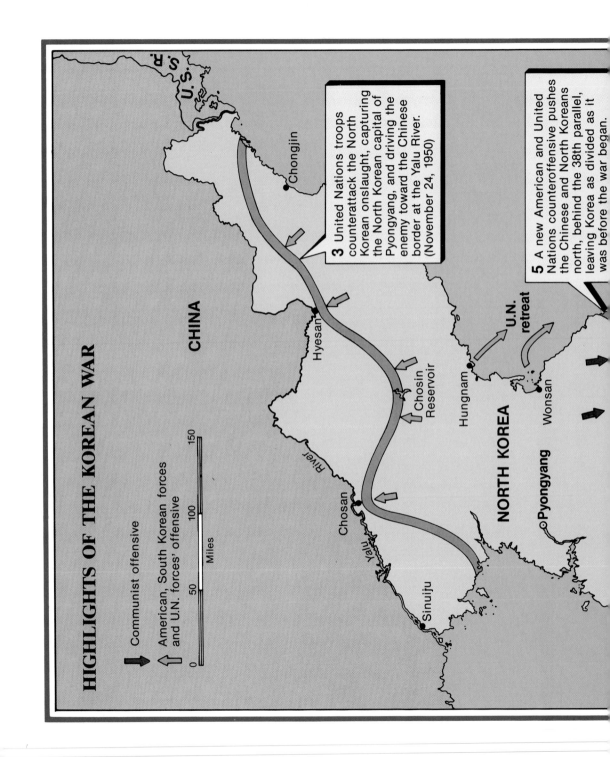

HIGHLIGHTS OF THE KOREAN WAR

Communist offensive

American, South Korean forces and U.N. forces' offensive

Miles

0   50   100   150

CHINA

U.S.S.R.

Chongjin

3 United Nations troops counterattack the North Korean onslaught, capturing the North Korean capital of Pyongyang, and driving the enemy toward the Chinese border at the Yalu River. (November 24, 1950)

Hyesan

Chosin Reservoir

Yalu River

Chosan

Sinuiju

U.N. retreat

Hungnam

Wonsan

5 A new American and United Nations counteroffensive pushes the Chinese and North Koreans north, behind the 38th parallel, leaving Korea as divided as it was before the war began.

NORTH KOREA

○**Pyongyang**

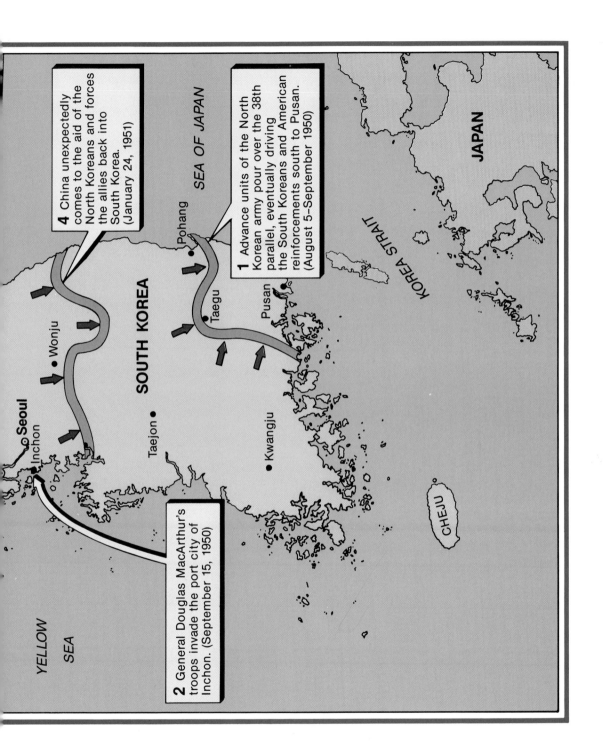

4 China unexpectedly comes to the aid of the North Koreans and forces the allies back into South Korea. (January 24, 1951)

1 Advance units of the North Korean army pour over the 38th parallel, eventually driving the South Koreans and American reinforcements south to Pusan. (August 5–September 1950)

2 General Douglas MacArthur's troops invade the port city of Inchon. (September 15, 1950)

YELLOW SEA

SEA OF JAPAN

KOREA STRAIT

JAPAN

SOUTH KOREA

Seoul
Inchon
Wonju
Taejon
Pohang
Taegu
Pusan
Kwangju

CHEJU

The shattered North Korean army, having abandoned most of its tanks and large weapons in the south, collapsed in the face of this invasion. Thousands of soldiers surrendered, scores more escaped to the north, seeking refuge in China. By October 19 the North Korean capital, Pyongyang, had been captured by UN troops and the North Korean government had fled. It appeared as if the "Korean Police Action" was about over. American soldiers began to talk hopefully about being home for Christmas.

But then there was a sudden and unpleasant surprise for the UN army. ROK units moving near the Yalu River, which forms a large portion of the border between China and North Korea, suddenly found themselves in combat with Chinese soldiers. Moving at night so that they wouldn't be seen by U.S. airplanes, four Chinese armies—about 130,000 men—had crossed bridges over the Yalu and now occupied the mountainous regions of North Korea. They were commanded by General Peng Dehuai, one of China's most capable leaders of the civil war; they called themselves "the Chinese People's Volunteers."

The Chinese were not nearly as well equipped as the UN soldiers. Their rifles and machine guns were mainly World War II weapons taken from Japanese troops that had surrendered at the end of the war. They had no large artillery pieces and no tanks. They had hardly any trucks—most of their supplies of food and ammunition were carried on the backs of men, in 100-pound (45 kg) bundles! But most of the Chinese had been soldiers for more than five years. They were skilled and experienced in warfare, used to hardship and discomfort, and not afraid to risk their lives. The ROK soldiers were no match for them.

On October 15 General MacArthur had assured President Truman that China would not enter the war, and now MacArthur and other American generals couldn't believe the reports they were getting; they couldn't believe that China had really come into the conflict. They thought that the Chinese soldiers the ROK troops had encountered were probably only a few thousand volunteers who had come to help the North Koreans. But as it became clear that the ROK units were being overwhelmed and destroyed by these "volunteers," General Walker ordered a U.S. division forward to push the Chinese back over the Yalu. Also, squadrons of American planes took to the sky to scout and attack the Chinese forces.

The troops of the American division pursuing the Chinese soon found themselves in heavy combat. The Chinese launched savage attacks, often at night. American soldiers were suddenly jolted out of sleep by sounds of shrill whistles, blaring bugles, drums, shouting voices, and the sharp cracks of rifle fire. Bewildered and half-asleep, they struggled to their feet, suddenly becoming aware of swarms of yelling Chinese soldiers all around them.

Shots exploded on all sides, and the Americans realized the Chinese were slicing right through them, and swinging

The bodies of South Korean civilians killed
by retreating North Korean forces are unearthed
in Pyongyang, three days after the North Korean
capital was captured by UN troops.
Facing page, top: Armed troops of the Chinese
People's Volunteers march through the North
Korean city of Kaesong. At bottom is
General Peng Dehuai (with pen),
their commander.

around to come at them from behind and from the sides. In sudden panic that they would be cut off, trapped, and captured, Americans began to dash to the rear, hoping to escape, hoping to find a place where they could turn around and fight back. But the Chinese had managed to split them into small groups, and many Americans were killed or captured.

More UN troops were sent forward, but these, too, ran into vicious attacks and had to pull back. By November 16 it was clear that the UN army was in serious trouble; its forward movement had been stopped, and it was being pushed back. It seemed unable to hold back the Chinese.

Then, suddenly and strangely, the Chinese stopped attacking. They pulled back into the mountains of North Korea and seemed to vanish!

FIVE

A CRISIS

IT WAS as if the Chinese had given a warning—we can beat you, do not come any farther. But American leaders did not know what to make of the situation. Some felt the Chinese had had to pull back because they were actually beaten. General MacArthur decided to disregard what had happened and continue with his plan to conquer all of North Korea.

The Tenth Corps, which had made the landing at Inchon, had been sent up along the east coast of North Korea, and on November 24, 1950, MacArthur ordered the Eighth Army to also move forward again. For the first twenty-four hours nothing happened. Then, without warning, the Chinese struck; they had received reinforcements. The Eighth Army was hit on its right flank by a massive attack of some 180,000 Chinese troops.

Once again, young American soldiers were startled out of their sleep by the blaring bugles and shrill whistles that characterized a Chinese night attack. The U.S. Second Infantry Division lost 4,000 men and most of its artillery pieces while fighting its way back out of hordes of Chinese troops attempting to surround it. A Turkish brigade that was now part of the UN army also had to fight its way out of encirclement. The Eighth Army began to retreat.

In the east, the Tenth Corps suddenly found itself under attack by 120,000 Chinese soldiers. The Third and Seventh Infantry Divisions managed to pull back to the coastal ports of Hungnam and Wonsan, but the First Marine Division was cut off and surrounded by eight Chinese divisions. The bitter Korean winter had now set in, and for thirteen days in freezing, below-zero weather, the marines fought their way through to Hungnam. The encounter came to be known as the Battle of the Chosin Reservoir. At MacArthur's orders, navy ships had assembled at the two ports, which U.S. troops managed to hold despite constant attacks. By December 15 all the Tenth Corps troops, together with thousands of vehicles, tons of supplies, and almost 100,000 civilian refugees, were evacuated by sea.

By this time, the Eighth Army had retreated all the way back below the 38th parallel, out of North Korea. The UN force, and particularly the U.S. troops, had suffered disastrous defeat and were now facing the onslaught of both the

Units of the North Korean People's Army
and the Chinese People's Volunteers
celebrate their joint defeat of
an attack by U.S. forces.

Chinese army and North Korean troops, which were advancing toward the South Korean border.

On December 23, General Walker's jeep, racing along an icy road, collided with a ROK army weapons carrier (a tank-like vehicle), and Walker was killed. Four days later, Lieutenant General Matthew Ridgway of the U.S. Army was appointed to command the UN ground forces in Korea. After flying to Korea from the United States, Ridgway found the American troops dispirited, sullen, and poorly disciplined, with no desire to win the war and with only the hope of being evacuated from Korea as soon as possible. He set about making changes at once; General Ridgway visited individual units and gave "pep talks," replacing incompetent officers, reorganizing, and rebuilding discipline. The troops began to respond.

On January 4, 1951, UN forces had to pull out of Seoul as the Chinese army approached. Once again the South Korean capital was in enemy hands. Then, in a long battle that lasted

Facing the coldest winter of the decade, the First Marine Division staged a courageous retreat from the Chosin Reservoir. There, they unwittingly walked into a trap and were overwhelmingly surrounded by Chinese troops.

Scenes from the Korean War. *Clockwise, from top left:* Marines trudge forward after U.S. air units have bombed enemy positions on the hillside. U.S. soldiers hiding in a cave are discovered and captured by members of the Chinese People's Volunteers. U.S. soldiers assault a North Korean bunker. A wounded marine is carried to a clearing station for treatment.

from January 8 to 15, American troops, strengthened by Ridgway's leadership, stopped the Chinese advance.

Actually, the Chinese were in extremely poor condition. They were running short of food and ammunition, their uniforms were not suited to the dreadful cold of the Korean winter, and a great number were suffering from frostbite. Wearing boots and items of clothing taken from dead and captured American soldiers, many of them were living off captured American food supplies.

On March 13 the Chinese began to pull back. On March 15 revitalized American troops and their UN allies recaptured Seoul. By April 3 the UN army had crossed the 38th parallel and moved back into North Korea.

But now, trouble was brewing between General MacArthur and the political leaders of the nations making up the UN army. MacArthur was angered that the Chinese were free to make preparations for warfare in safety on their side of the border. He wanted to carry the war into China, bombing the areas across the border where Chinese troops were organized and supplied for their movement into Korea. President Truman and the leaders of Britain and other European nations were horrified by such a suggestion; they felt that if China itself were attacked, the Soviet Union would surely join the war and World War III would begin.

The UN leaders insisted warfare had to be limited only to Korea. MacArthur disagreed, and when he publicly criticized President Truman for going along with this "limited

General Matthew Ridgway succeeded
General MacArthur as the supreme
commander of the UN troops.

war" idea, Truman, in his capacity as commander in chief of U.S. military forces, removed MacArthur from command and appointed General Ridgway as supreme commander in his place. United States general James van Fleet became commander of the ground forces in Korea.

On April 22 the Chinese launched an attack that halted the UN advance and pushed it back. But the U.S. and UN troops had more confidence now, and their defense stiffened. On May 22 General van Fleet ignited a counterattack supported by tremendous amounts of artillery fire directed at Chinese positions. The Chinese army was now in extremely bad condition. All their earlier successes and victories in pushing the UN forces back had been won at the expense of vast casualties; they had lost some 200,000 men in the last six months. They had also used up most of their supplies. They began to rapidly pull back.

Apparently fearing that Chinese and North Korean forces might now suddenly collapse, leaving all of Korea securely in non-Communist hands, the Soviet government ordered its ambassador to the UN to call for a cease-fire, a halt to the fighting. The Chinese government let word leak out that it too desired a cease-fire. On June 29, General Ridgway offered to meet the Chinese and North Korean commanders to discuss a cease-fire and armistice (an agreement to end the war). Several days later the Communists agreed. Peace talks began on July 10 at a city called Kaesong, in South Korea, a few miles from the 38th parallel.

SIX
THE
"TALKING WAR"
AND AN
UNEASY PEACE

WHILE the UN and Communist commanders were trying to work out the terms of peace, the fighting continued. But battles were now fought mainly to try to give one side or the other an advantage in the peace talks. American and UN troops, as well as young Chinese and North Korean soldiers, died in meaningless combat over hills that became known as "Bloody Ridge" and "Heartbreak Ridge." United Nations soldiers bitterly referred to the period of the peace talks as the "talking war."

The talks and the spurts of fighting dragged on for month after month. After nearly two years, the United States government, now headed by President Dwight D. Eisenhower, let it be known that it would directly engage China in war, if necessary, to get the Communists to finally come to some agreement. On May 28, 1953, the UN negotiators at the peace talks presented their final terms and threatened to break off the meetings and resume full-scale warfare if the terms were

Left: President Dwight D. Eisenhower (left) chats with General James van Fleet, commander of the ground forces in Korea.

Below: The Korean armistice was signed by senior delegates representing the United Nations (left) and the Communist Group (right) in Panmunjom.

rejected. Almost two months later, on July 27, an armistice was finally signed.

Technically, the war was over; but actually, an armistice is merely an agreement to stop fighting until a permanent peace treaty is signed—but a peace treaty has never been signed between North and South Korea, nor between any of the nations that had opposing forces in Korea. There is still tension between North and South Korea, and over the years since 1953, there have been brief outbursts of fighting in the 2.5-mile-deep (4 km) stretch of open, neutral land that was set up between the north and the south borders as a result of the peace talks. As of 1991, there were still many thousands of U.S. soldiers stationed in South Korea to prevent another invasion from *either* direction.

The South Korean army suffered 58,127 deaths during the war; the United States, 54,246 deaths; and the forces of the other fourteen UN members in the war, a total of 3,194 deaths. There were also nearly 300,000 men wounded, of which 175,743 were South Korean and 103,284 American. It is estimated that the North Korean and Chinese forces suffered nearly 1.5 million dead and wounded soldiers.

But after all these casualties, and after three years of fighting that destroyed most of the major cities of North and South Korea and killed and injured millions of North and South Korean civilians, the situation was almost exactly the same as it had been when the war started—one country

The vestiges of war. *Clockwise, from top left:* Chinese Communist soldiers are rounded up as prisoners of war. Thousands of peasants were uprooted from their homes as they fled the Communists bearing down on their land. War orphans wander through the ruins of Seoul. A Korean girl places a wreath of flowers on the grave of an American soldier at the UN cemetary in Pusan.

Far from home: a military policeman guards his post next to signs showing the distance between U.S. cities and Seoul.

A divided Korea.
Top: North Korean students sketch at a park in the nation's capital of Pyongyang. *Bottom:* South Koreans celebrate the blossoming of 70,000 cherry trees during the annual Chinhae Cherry Blossom Festival.

divided into two separate nations, one Communist and one non-Communist. The new dividing line, based on the battle line at the time the peace talks began, gave a slight increase of territory to South Korea.

Although the Korean War did not seem to have changed things much, it had a deep effect on much of the world. It made China into a major world power. It caused the United States, which had disbanded most of its military forces after World War II, to rearm and become the major military power of the Western world, bringing about great changes in the American way of life. It increased a fear and loathing of communism among most Americans and many Europeans, leading to decades of dangerous confrontation and hostility between the United States and the Soviet Union, which is only now beginning to subside.

The Korean War was also the first time in history in which a number of nations banded together to prevent one nation from forcibly taking over another and changing its way of life. Although the Republic of Korea has never quite been a true democracy, today it is a bustling, modestly wealthy nation with a decent standard of living for most of its people. Had the United States and its UN allies not moved at once to halt North Korea's aggression, the situation in South Korea might now be far different.

BIBLIOGRAPHY

Alexander, Bevin. *Korea: The First War We Lost.* New York: Hippocrene Books, 1986.

Blair, Clay. *The Forgotten War: America in Korea, 1950–1953.* New York: Times Books, 1987.

DuPuy, R. Ernest, and Trevor N. DuPuy. *The Encyclopedia of Military History.* New York: Harper & Row, 1977.

Foot, Rosemary. *The Wrong War: American Policy and the Dimensions of the Korean Conflict, 1950–1953.* Ithaca, N.Y.: Cornell University Press, 1985.

Goulden, Joseph C. *Korea: The Untold Story of the War.* New York: Times Books, 1982.

Hastings, Max. *The Korean War.* New York: Simon and Schuster, 1987.

Hoyt, Edwin P. *The Bloody Road to Panmunjom*. New York: Stein and Day, 1985.

Knox, Donald. *The Korean War: Pusan to Chosin. An Oral History.* New York: Harcourt Brace Jovanovich, 1985.

Spurr, Russell. *Enter the Dragon: China's Undeclared War Against the U.S. in Korea, 1950–53*. New York: Newmarket Press, 1988.

INDEX

Page numbers in *italics* refer to illustrations.

ABOUT THE AUTHOR

"I LIVED through the Korean War as a young man," says Tom McGowen, an avid fan of military history and a veteran of World War II, which had concluded only five years prior to the outbreak of the Korean War. As a result, the author became thoroughly familiar with the weaponry and tactics of the period, as well as with the frame of mind of the fighting men of the time.

Mr. McGowen is the author of over thirty-five books for young people. In 1986 his book *Radioactivity: From the Curies to the Atomic Age* (Franklin Watts) was named an NSTA-CBC Outstanding Science Trade Book for Children. *The Great Monkey Trial: Science Versus Fundamentalism in America,* a book he recently wrote for Franklin Watts's Twentieth Century American History series, was cited in a pointer review in *Kirkus* as "a fascinating, well-organized account."

Mr. McGowen lives with his wife, Loretta, in Norridge, Illinois.